For Leo and Francesca
L.C.

British Library Cataloguing in Publication Data

Listen to this
1. Children's stories, English
I. Cecil, Laura   II. Clark, Emma Chichester
823'.01'089282   PZ5

ISBN 0-370-31100-0

This compilation copyright © Laura Cecil 1987
Illustrations copyright © Emma Chichester Clark 1987
Photoset by Rowland Phototypesetting Ltd
Bury St Edmunds, Suffolk
Printed in Great Britain for
The Bodley Head Ltd
32 Bedford Square, London WC1B 3EL
by William Clowes Ltd, Beccles, Suffolk
First published 1987

Introduction

As I work in children's books, people often ask me what kind of story is a success with young children. There is no simple answer, but I have come to think that part of it lies in how children experience reading in their everyday lives. Young children associate reading with certain places and moments in the day. These are usually the story at bedtime, the visit to the library, or storytime at school, where an adult reads to them. In this way reading becomes a ritual; but it is also a social occasion for children where they respond to the story and the storyteller at the same time. This makes the experience unlike that of adults reading to themselves, but it has much in common with storytelling where the cultural tradition is oral rather than literary. I think this explains why folktales, though originally told to adults, have such an appeal to children. For this reason the children's stories I have found most successful have been those which most closely recreate the experience of hearing an individual tell a story first hand.

I did not set out to demonstrate this when I started my selection. My aim at first was to find stories that would appeal to a child's imagination, and give adults pleasure to read. But as the collection grew it became clear that the oral tradition had a strong influence on my choice. All the stories, whether actual folktales or new ones, have been written to be heard rather than read, and in many cases were originally told by the writer before being written down. Several are the result of storytelling to the writers' own children. Kipling first told the *Just So Stories* to his eldest daughter, Josephine. There is still the intimate quality of private references and jokes to be found in 'How the Rhinoceros Got his Skin', with its domestic details about the Parsee's cooking-stove "of the kind that you must particularly never touch" and the lists of exotic place names. The style surely comes from Kipling's own childhood listening to stories in India, where the oral tradition was alive then as now. Partap Sharma's story, 'Ghabru and the Little Lie', also derives from this tradition.

Richard Hughes perhaps gets closest to a child's experience of storytelling outside books. He improvised his stories to children, often in large groups, with some of the ingredients of the story contributed by the children themselves. If the story was a success, the following day Hughes would ask a child to tell it back to him and he would write it down. 'The Elephant's Picnic' as a result captures that unfettered fantasy and surreal humour that are so characteristic of spontaneous storytelling.

The stories vary in mood and subject and none of them could be termed "realistic". Each has at least one fantastic element whether it is a talking wolf or a horse made out of cake. Fantasy has always been at the heart of storytelling because it provides something extraordinary to catch the attention and imagination of the listeners. It also enables the teller to express an idea in an entertaining way, even when it is a disturbing one. This is particularly effective when telling a story to children. The Mr Miacca of Jacobs' fairytale was a traditional bogeyman invented to warn naughty children; in this case not to wander off on their own or they might be taken by a stranger. Philippa Pearce's 'Lion at School' deals with the fears children have of playground bullies.

My choice has tended towards humour, as this is especially enjoyable to read aloud. The power to make someone laugh, even if it is reading someone else's joke, is always gratifying and the uninhibited response of children most gratifying of all. Absurd names, like those the cat uses for her imaginary godchildren in 'The Cat and the Mouse in Partnership' or absurd sounds used in 'The Biggest Cream Bun in the World', have an instant delighted reaction. I have also chosen stories that have an individual voice, whether it is that of a known writer, or expresses a folk tradition, such as the black American story, 'A Wolf and Little Daughter'. Contrary to what might be expected, this makes them easier to read aloud as the reader is able to enter into the spirit of the story, like an actor donning a character in a play.

All these stories work well when read aloud; but I know that children respond as much to the illustrations in a book. I have not given an illustrator an easy task as the stories are unconnected in period and subject matter except for the common element of fantasy. So I have found it most exciting to see how Emma Chichester Clark's fresh and vivid imagination has responded to the stories and given them a visual unity. The result is irresistible.

Laura Cecil
February 1987

Contents

The Elephant's Picnic
RICHARD HUGHES

Elephants are generally clever animals, but there was once an elephant who was very silly; and his great friend was a kangaroo. Now, kangaroos are not often clever animals, and this one certainly was not, so she and the elephant got on very well together.

One day they thought they would like to go off for a picnic by themselves. But they did not know anything about picnics, and had not the faintest idea of what to do to get ready.

"What do you do on a picnic?" the elephant asked a child he knew.

"Oh, we collect wood and make a fire, and then we boil the kettle," said the child.

"What do you boil the kettle for?" said the elephant in surprise.

"Why, for tea, of course," said the child in a snapping sort of way; so the elephant did not like to ask any more questions. But he went and told the kangaroo, and they collected together all the things they thought they would need.

When they got to the place where they were going to have their picnic, the kangaroo said that she would collect the wood because she had got a pouch to carry it back in. A kangaroo's pouch, of course, is very small; so the kangaroo carefully chose the smallest twigs she could find, and only about five or six of those. In fact, it took a lot of hopping to find any sticks small enough to go in her pouch at all; and it was a long time before she came back. But silly though the elephant was, he soon saw those sticks would not be enough for a fire.

"Now *I* will go off and get some wood," he said.

His ideas of getting wood were very different. Instead of taking little twigs he pushed down whole trees with his forehead, and staggered back to the picnic-place with them rolled up in his trunk. Then the kangaroo struck a match, and they lit a bonfire made of whole trees. The blaze, of course, was enormous, and the fire so hot that for a long time they could not get near it; and it was not until it began to die down a bit that they were able to get near enough to cook anything.

"Now let's boil the kettle," said the elephant. Amongst the things he had brought was a brightly shining copper kettle and a very large black iron saucepan. The elephant filled the saucepan with water.

"What are you doing that for?" said the kangaroo.

"To boil the kettle in, you silly," said the elephant. So he popped the kettle in the saucepan of water, and put the saucepan on the fire; for he thought, the old juggins, that you boil a kettle in the same sort of way you boil an egg, or boil a cabbage! And the kangaroo, of course, did not know any better.

So they boiled and boiled the kettle, and every now and then they prodded it with a stick.

"It doesn't seem to be getting tender," said the elephant sadly, "and I am sure we can't eat it for tea until it does."

So then away he went and got more wood for the fire; and still the saucepan boiled and boiled, and still the kettle remained as hard as ever. It was getting late now, almost dark.

"I am afraid it won't be ready for tea," said the kangaroo. "I am afraid we shall have to spend the night here. I wish we had got something with us to sleep in."

"Haven't you?" said the elephant. "You mean to say you didn't pack before you came away?"

"No," said the kangaroo. "What should I have packed, anyway?"

"Why, your trunk, of course," said the elephant. "That is what people pack."

"But I haven't got a trunk," said the kangaroo.

"Well, I have," said the elephant, "and I've packed it. Kindly pass the pepper; I want to unpack!"

So then the kangaroo passed the elephant the pepper, and the elephant took a good sniff. Then he gave a most enormous sneeze, and everything he had packed in his trunk shot out of

it—toothbrush, spare socks, gym shoes, a comb, a bag of bull's-eyes, his pyjamas, and his Sunday suit. So then the elephant put on his pyjamas and lay down to sleep; but the kangaroo had no pyjamas, and so, of course, she could not possibly sleep.

"All right," she said to the elephant, "you sleep and I will sit up and keep the fire going."

So all night the kangaroo kept the fire blazing brightly and the kettle boiling merrily in the saucepan. When the next morning came, the elephant woke up.

"Now," he said, "let's have our breakfast."

So they took the kettle out of the saucepan; and what do you think? *It was boiled as tender as tender could be!* So they cut it fairly in half and shared it between them, and ate it for their breakfast; and both agreed they had never had so good a breakfast in their lives.

How the Rhinoceros Got his Skin
RUDYARD KIPLING

Once upon a time, on an uninhabited island on the shores of the Red Sea, there lived a Parsee from whose hat the rays of the sun were reflected in more-than-oriental splendour. And the Parsee lived by the Red Sea with nothing but his hat and his knife and a cooking-stove of the kind that you must particularly never touch. And one day he took flour and water and currants and plums and sugar and things, and made himself one cake which was two feet across and three feet thick. It was indeed a Superior Comestible (*that's* Magic), and he put it on the stove because *he* was allowed to cook on that stove, and he baked it and he baked it till it was all done brown and smelt most sentimental. But just as he was going to eat it there came down to the beach from the Altogether Uninhabited Interior one Rhinoceros with a horn on his nose, two piggy eyes, and few manners. In those days the Rhinoceros's skin fitted him quite tight. There were no wrinkles in it anywhere. He looked exactly like a Noah's Ark Rhinoceros, but of course much bigger. All the same, he had no manners then, and he has no manners now, and he never will have any

manners. He said, "How!" and the Parsee left that cake and climbed to the top of a palm-tree with nothing on but his hat, from which the rays of the sun were always reflected in more-than-oriental splendour. And the Rhinoceros upset the oil-stove with his nose, and the cake rolled on the sand,

and he spiked that cake on the horn of his nose, and he ate it, and he went away, waving his tail, to the desolate and Exclusively Uninhabited Interior which abuts on the islands of Mazanderan, Socotra, and the Promontories of the Larger Equinox. Then the Parsee came down from his palm-tree and put the stove on its legs and recited the following *Sloka*, which, as you have not heard, I will now proceed to relate:

Them that takes cakes
which the Parsee man bakes
makes DREADFUL mistakes

And there was a great deal more in that than you would think.

Because, five weeks later, there was a heatwave in the Red Sea, and everybody took off all the clothes they had. The Parsee took off his hat; but the Rhinoceros took off his skin and carried it over his shoulder as he came down to the beach to bathe. In those days it buttoned underneath with three buttons and looked like a waterproof. He said nothing whatever about the Parsee's cake, because he had eaten it all; and he never had any manners, then, since, or henceforward. He waddled straight into the water and blew bubbles through his nose, leaving his skin on the beach.

Presently the Parsee came by and found the skin, and he smiled one smile that ran all round his face two times. Then he danced three times round the skin and rubbed his hands. Then he went to his camp and filled his hat with cake-crumbs, for the Parsee never ate anything but cake, and never swept out his camp. He took that skin, and he shook that skin, and he scrubbed that skin, and he rubbed that skin just as full of old, dry, stale, tickly cake-crumbs and some burned currants as ever it could *possibly* hold. Then he climbed to the top of his palm-tree and waited for the Rhinoceros to come out of the water and put it on.

And the Rhinoceros did. He buttoned it up with the three buttons, and it tickled like cake-crumbs in bed. Then he wanted to scratch, but that made it worse; and then he lay down on the sands and rolled and rolled and rolled, and every time he rolled the cake-crumbs tickled him worse and worse and worse. Then he ran to the palm-tree and rubbed and rubbed and rubbed himself against it. He rubbed so much and so hard that he rubbed his skin into a great fold over his shoulders, and another fold underneath, where the buttons used to be (but he rubbed the buttons off), and he rubbed some more folds over his legs. And it spoiled his temper, but it didn't make the least difference to the cake-crumbs. They were inside his skin and they tickled. So he went home, very angry indeed and horribly scratchy; and from that day to this every rhinoceros has great folds in his skin and a very bad temper, all on account of the cake-crumbs inside.

But the Parsee came down from his palm-tree, wearing his hat, from which the rays of the sun were reflected in more-than-oriental splendour, packed up his cooking-stove, and went away in the direction of Orotavo, Amygdala, the Upland Meadows of Anantarivo, and the Marshes of Sonaput.

The Biggest Cream Bun in the World

MARY CALVERT

Big Fat Rosie was the biggest, fattest person there ever was.

She was bigger than a barrel.

She was plumper than a pudding.

She was rounder than a rubber ball.

And almost as heavy as a medium-sized hippopotamus.

And Big Fat Rosie was very, very wide. She was so wide that:

She had to sit on an extra-wide chair.

She had to sleep in an extra-wide bed.

She had to eat with an extra-wide spoon.

And all the doors in her house were extra-extra wide, so that she could move from room to room without getting stuck.

Everything that Big Fat Rosie did was done enormously. When she ate (with her extra-wide spoon), she made a noise like this

ompa chompa ompa chompa

When she slept (in her extra-wide bed), she snored like this

cor-fyoo o o o
    cor-fyoo o°o°o

and all the walls quivered.

When she cried, like this

owo -wo -wo
owo -wo -wo

such huge tears fell from her eyes that everything around her became soaking wet.

Big Fat Rosie was a farmer's wife, and her husband was called Turnip Tom. While Rosie looked after the house, Turnip Tom managed everything around the farm. He had pigs and cows and ducks and chickens and he grew wheat, cabbages, potatoes and, of course, turnips. Turnip Tom was very good to Big Fat Rosie and bought her plenty of nice things to eat. This made Big Fat Rosie happy, because she was very greedy indeed—and her favourite food was cream buns.

One day, when Turnip Tom was out working in the fields, Big Fat Rosie thought she would give him a surprise. She would make a great big cream bun and they could eat it together for their tea. She giggled happily, like this

Ki Ki Ki Ki

and made a list of all the things she would need: flour, eggs, milk, butter, sugar and cream.

There were big bags of flour and sugar in the larder, but the other ingredients would have to be collected from the farm.

Big Fat Rosie put on her rubber farm boots and went first to the cowshed, where Old Harry, the farm-boy, was putting hay in the cows' manger. Outside, the cows made hungry, waiting noises, like this

"Hallo, Harry," said Big Fat Rosie. "Please may I have some milk and some butter and some cream? I'm going to make the biggest cream bun in the world."

"Arr," said Harry, scratching his head. "When a bun's big as that, there'll be some as gets fat."

"Yes," agreed Rosie, laughing cosily, "me." (Because, of course, she was already as fat as a couple of eiderdowns.)

Harry went into the dairy and came out with a can of milk, a bowl of butter and a jug of cream. Big Fat Rosie thanked him and trotted off towards the henhouse to look for some eggs.

When the hens saw her, they made a fearful racket, like this

cookerookeroo
cookerookeroo
roo

and flapped about her feet.

"No, no!" cried Big Fat Rosie. "It isn't tea-time yet. I've come to fetch some eggs." She went over to the nesting boxes and looked inside. There were ten beautiful speckly-brown eggs, some of them still warm. She put them in her apron pocket and walked carefully back to the farmhouse, trying not to bump them with her knees. "Hee hee!" she thought. "Now I can make the biggest cream bun in the world!"

When the mixture was ready in the bowl, Big Fat Rosie stirred it with her wooden spoon, like this

slurrp slurrp

and licked her lips. She tasted the mixture twenty-six times, just to be sure it was right, and added a few spoonfuls of yeast. Yeast would make the bun rise splendidly, like a loaf of bread. Turnip Tom *would* be pleased.

Big Fat Rosie bent down to light the oven. It made a noise like this

POP POP

and she poured the bun mixture on to the biggest baking tray she could find. When she had placed it in the oven, she sat in her very wide rocking chair and hummed a little happy tune as she rocked, like this

dum dum di dum dumetty dumetty dum

And then she fell asleep.

In the oven, the bun was rising higher and higher. In the chair, Rosie was snoring louder and louder, like this

cor-fyoo cor-fyoo

The whole kitchen was shaking with the noise—until suddenly the oven door burst open with a bang. Big Fat Rosie woke up, rubbed her eyes and looked around her. What on earth was that peculiar sound? It went like this

Splobble Splobble

It was the bun! It was pouring out of the oven! Over the floor
it crept steadily, blobbing and bubbling, slopping and slurping.

It looked as though it would never stop. But Big Fat Rosie was not going to be beaten by a bun. She knew she could never sweep it up—but she could eat it. It was almost time for tea, anyway. She grabbed the nearest piece and began to eat very fast, like this

ompa chompa ompa chompa

But the bun kept on coming. It was rising up the table legs and Big Fat Rosie had to eat even faster, like this

ompa chompa ompa chompa

She wished she had never put all that yeast in the mixture.

Then the bun began to creep over the window sill and out into the garden. Turnip Tom, coming home from the fields, called out to Harry.

"Come quick! There's a bun climbing out of the window!"

"Dearie me," said Harry and hurried with him to the kitchen. There they found Big Fat Rosie knee deep in bun, eating more and more slowly, like this

om-pah-chom-pah

"Omp," she mumbled, almost in tears. "It was going—omp—to be the biggest chomp bomp in the womp."

"Never mind," said Turnip Tom, who always knew exactly what to do, "Harry and I can take it away in a barrow."

"Arr," said Harry.

They fetched their shovels and a wheelbarrow and began to scrape the cream bun off the walls. Harry switched off the oven and the rest of the dough began to sink.

Finally, it stopped. Turnip Tom gave a great big sigh of relief, like this

whee-yew

and stood looking thoughtfully at the barrowload of bun. "We could bury it in the garden," he suggested.

Harry said: "When a bun gets too big, remember the pig."

So they gave the bun to Alexander, who was always hungry, and he grunted happily, like this

oinker oinker oink

as if to say "Thank you very much."

But Big Fat Rosie thought he was saying "What a rotten cook" and decided she would make another biggest cream bun in the world tomorrow, just to show him. And this time it would be even bigger.

Lion at School
PHILIPPA PEARCE

Once upon a time there was a little girl who didn't like going to school. She always set off late. Then she had to hurry, but she never hurried fast enough.

One morning she was hurrying along as usual when she turned a corner and there stood a lion, blocking her way. He stood waiting for her. He stared at her with his yellow eyes. He

growled, and when he growled, the little girl could see that his teeth were as sharp as skewers and knives. He growled, "I'm going to eat you up."

"Oh, dear!" said the little girl, and she began to cry.

"Wait!" said the lion. "I haven't finished. I'm going to eat you up UNLESS you take me to school with you."

35

"Oh, dear!" said the little girl. "I couldn't do that. My teacher says we mustn't bring pets to school."

"I'm not a pet," said the lion. He growled again, and she saw that his tail swished from side to side in anger—*swish! swash!* "You can tell your teacher that I'm a friend who is coming to school with you," he said. "Now shall we go?"

The little girl had stopped crying. She said, "All right. But you must promise two things. First of all, you mustn't eat anyone; it's not allowed."

"I suppose I can growl?" said the lion.

"I suppose you can," said the little girl.

"And I suppose I can roar?"

"Must you?" said the little girl.

"Yes," said the lion.

"Then I suppose you can," said the little girl.

"And what's the second thing?" asked the lion.

"You must let me ride on your back to school."

"Very well," said the lion.

He crouched down on the pavement and the little girl climbed on to his back. She held on by his mane. Then they went on together towards the school, the little girl riding the lion.

The lion ran with the little girl on his back to school. Even so, they were late. The little girl and the lion went into the classroom just as the teacher was calling the register.

The teacher stopped calling the register when she saw the little girl and the lion. She stared at the lion, and all the other children stared at the lion, wondering what the teacher was going to say. The teacher said to the little girl, "You know you are not allowed to bring pets to school."

The lion began to swish his tail—*swish! swash!* The little girl said, "This is not a pet. This is my friend who is coming to school with me."

The teacher still stared at the lion, but she said to the little girl, "What is his name then?"

"Noil," said the little girl. "His name is Noil. Just Noil." She knew it would be no good to tell the teacher that her friend was a lion, so she had turned his name backwards: LION—NOIL.

The teacher wrote the name down in the register: NOIL. Then she finished calling the register.

"Betty Small," she said.

"Yes," said the little girl.

"Noil," said the teacher.

"Yes," said the lion. He mumbled, opening his mouth as little as possible, so that the teacher should not see his teeth as sharp as skewers and knives.

All that morning the lion sat up on his chair next to the little girl, like a big cat, with his tail curled around his front paws, as good as gold. He didn't speak unless the teacher spoke to him. He didn't growl; he didn't roar.

At playtime the little girl and the lion went into the playground. All the children stopped playing to stare at the lion. Then they went on playing again. The little girl stood in a corner of the playground, with the lion beside her.

"Why don't we play like the others?" the lion asked.

The little girl said, "I don't like playing because some of the big boys are so big and rough. They knock you over without meaning to."

The lion growled. "They wouldn't knock ME over," he said.

"There's one big boy—the very biggest," said the little girl. "His name is Jack Tall. He knocks me over on purpose."

"Which is he?" said the lion. "Point him out to me."

38

The little girl pointed out Jack Tall to the lion.

"Ah!" said the lion. "So that's Jack Tall."

Just then the bell rang again, and all the children went back to their classrooms. The lion went with the little girl and sat beside her.

Then the children drew and wrote until dinnertime. The lion was hungry, so he wanted to draw a picture of his dinner.

"What will it be for dinner?" he asked the little girl. "I hope it's meat."

"No," said the little girl. "It will be fish fingers because today is Friday."

Then the little girl showed the lion how to hold the yellow crayon in his paw and draw fish fingers. Underneath his picture

she wrote: "I like meat better than fish fingers."

Then it was dinnertime. The lion sat up on his chair at the dinner table next to the little girl.

The lion ate very fast, and at the end he said, "I'm still hungry, and I wish it had been meat."

After dinner all the children went into the playground.

All the big boys were running about, and the very biggest boy, Jack Tall, came running towards the little girl. He was running in circles, closer and closer to the little girl.

"Go away," said the lion. "You might knock my friend over. Go away."

"Shan't," said Jack Tall. The little girl got behind the lion.

Jack Tall was running closer and closer and closer.

The lion growled. Then Jack Tall saw the lion's teeth as sharp as skewers and knives. He stopped running. He stood still. He stared.

The lion opened his mouth wider—so wide that Jack Tall could see his throat, opened wide and deep and dark like a tunnel to go into. Jack Tall went pale.

Then the lion roared.

He roared and he ROARED and he **ROARED**.

All the teachers came running out.

All the children stopped playing and stuck their fingers in their ears. And the biggest boy, Jack Tall, turned around and ran and ran and ran. He never stopped running until he got home to his mother.

The little girl came out from behind the lion. "Well," she

said, "I don't think much of *him*. I shall never be scared of *him* again."

"I was hungry," said the lion. "I could easily have eaten him. Only I'd promised you."

"And his mother wouldn't have liked it," said the little girl. "Time for afternoon school now."

"I'm not staying for afternoon school," said the lion.

"See you on Monday then," said the little girl. But the lion did not answer. He just walked off.

On Monday the lion did not come to school. At playtime, in the playground, the biggest boy came up to the little girl.

"Where's your friend that talks so loudly?" he said.

"He's not here today," said the little girl.

"Might he come another day?" asked the biggest boy.

"He might," said the little girl. "He easily might. So you just watch out, Jack Tall."

The Two Giraffes

JAMES REEVES

There were once two giraffes. They were married and were looking for a house to live in. Now the special thing about giraffes is that they are tall. This is useful to a giraffe when he wants to pick something high up in a tree or talk to the birds. But it is very awkward when he is looking for a house. Mr and Mrs Giraffe went to an office where they arrange about houses, and said:

"Please, we want to buy a house."

"I have nothing for the likes of you," said the man in the office. "You are too tall."

Then the two giraffes went to another office.

"Let us stoop down, my dear," said Mr Giraffe. "Let us make ourselves as small as possible."

They did this, and the man in the office, who was very superior, only laughed.

"Oh my, oh my!" he said. "The funniest thing I've seen for years is a giraffe trying to look small. I shall tell my wife about this. Sorry, I've nothing for you."

Then they went sadly along the street and saw a sign on a house, saying ROOMS TO LET.

"Well, if we can't buy a house," said Mrs Giraffe, "let's try to get some rooms."

They knocked at the door, and the landlady almost fell over backwards in surprise. But she was a polite landlady and when Mrs Giraffe asked if she could let them some rooms, she said:

"I'd have liked to, but I'm afraid you're too tall. You'd be hitting your heads on the ceiling all the time and smashing the electric lights. Besides, the other people might be surprised and upset. The only place you would be in any comfort would be on the staircase, and that wouldn't do at all. Have you tried the police station?"

"Oh, I don't think they'd want us in there," said Mr Giraffe. "Thank you all the same. We'll be on our way."

"We had better ask the King," said Mrs Giraffe. "It is his business to help us and all his citizens in distress. Let's go to the Palace."

When they got to the Palace, they found the gates guarded by two important-looking soldiers with fur helmets and guns slung on their shoulders.

"Who goes there?" said one of the sentries.

"Mr and Mrs Giraffe. We have come to see the King."

"Well, you can't," said the sentry. "He's out of town on an important state visit."

But the other sentry took pity on the two giraffes, seeing how tired and worried they looked.

"What is the trouble, Mr Giraffe?" he asked kindly. "Perhaps we could help you."

"We are rather tall," said Mr Giraffe, "and we can't find anywhere to live. It is not so bad wandering round in the daytime and walking in the park, but at night it is not nice to have no roof over our heads."

"Well, I can understand how you feel," said the sentry. "Me and my mate here are also very tall."

It was true. They were two of the tallest soldiers you ever saw, and with their fur helmets on they were almost as tall as the giraffes.

"In fact they had to build these two specially tall sentry-boxes for us, didn't they, Bill?"

"Yes," said his mate.

"Well, I'll tell you what we'll do," said the kind sentry. "While His Majesty's away, you can have our sentry-boxes to sleep in at night. We only use them during the day, and then only when it's raining. His Majesty doesn't like us to get our helmets wet. At night we don't use the boxes, because we have to patrol round the Palace. How about that?"

"Oh, that's very kind of you," said Mrs Giraffe. "It will certainly do until we can get ourselves a house the right size."

So that night, when the sentries were out on patrol, the two giraffes had the use of their tall boxes, which had high pointed roofs to put their heads under. This went on for several nights. Then one evening the sentries went to a party with some friends and quite forgot to go on duty in the Palace grounds.

45

Now it was on this very night that two robbers came to the Palace to steal some of the King's treasures while he was away on his important state visit. One of them was called Hugo, and the other wasn't. They crept up to the Palace gates with masks over their faces and pistols in their hands and a big sack labelled SWAG.

"You go first," said Hugo to his confederate.

"No, you go, Hugo," said the other, and Hugo went first. They always said this, and Hugo always went first.

"The sentries patrol the grounds at this time," said the one who wasn't called Hugo. "It's quite safe."

"Oh, is it?" said Hugo. "Then what's that in the sentry-boxes?"

When they saw the two tall spotted animals in the boxes, looking dim and terrible in the darkness, they gave a loud cry and dropped their pistols and their swag-bag. They took to their heels and ran—or rather, they took to their toes, for you can't run fast on your heels. Just you try it. The two robbers ran straight into the arms of the sentries, who had just woken up

and were coming at full speed to do their duty and guard the Palace.

They levelled their rifles and arrested the two robbers, who were speedily brought to justice.

The two tall sentries were so grateful to the giraffes for having frightened the robbers that they said they would tell the King when he came back, even though it meant owning up to being late on duty. The King was so pleased with Mr and Mrs Giraffe that he built them a tall house in the Royal Palace gardens and said they could live there as long as they liked, provided they did not frighten his friends. And that is how Mr and Mrs Giraffe got themselves a house to fit them.

A Wolf and Little Daughter
VIRGINIA HAMILTON

One day Little Daughter was pickin some flowers. There was a fence around the house she lived in with her papa. Papa didn't want Little Daughter to run in the forest, where there were wolves. He told Little Daughter never to go out the gate alone.

"Oh, I won't, Papa," said Little Daughter.

One mornin her papa had to go away for somethin. And Little Daughter thought she'd go huntin for flowers. She just thought it wouldn't harm anythin to peep through the gate. And that's what she did. She saw a wild yellow flower so near to the gate that she stepped outside and picked it.

Little Daughter was outside the fence now. She saw another pretty flower. She skipped over and got it, held it in her hand. It smelled sweet. She saw another and she got it, too. Put it with the others. She was makin a pretty bunch to put in her vase for the table. And so Little Daughter got farther and farther away from the cabin. She picked the flowers, and the whole time she sang a sweet song.

All at once Little Daughter heard a noise. She looked up and saw a great big wolf. The wolf said to her, in a low, gruff voice, said, "Sing that sweetest, goodest song again."

So the little child sang it, sang:

"*Tray-bla, tray-bla, cum qua, kimo.*"

And, *pit-a-pat, pit-a-pat, pit-a-pat, pit-a-pat*, Little Daughter tiptoed toward the gate. She's goin back home. But she hears big and heavy, PIT-A-PAT, PIT-A-PAT, comin behind her. And there's the wolf. He says, "Did you move?" in a gruff voice.

Little Daughter says, "Oh, no, dear wolf, what occasion have I to move?"

"Well, sing that sweetest, goodest song again," says the wolf.

Little Daughter sang it:

"*Tray-bla, tray-bla, cum qua, kimo.*"

And the wolf is gone again.

The child goes back some more, *pit-a-pat, pit-a-pat, pit-a-pat,* softly on tippy-toes toward the gate.

But she soon hears very loud, PIT-A-PAT, PIT-A-PAT, comin behind her. And there is the great big wolf, and he says to her, says, "I think you moved."

"Oh, no, dear wolf," Little Daughter tells him, "what occasion have I to move?"

51

So he says, "Sing that sweetest, goodest song again."

Little Daughter begins:

"Tray-bla, tray-bla, tray-bla, cum qua, kimo."

The wolf is gone.

But, PIT-A-PAT, PIT-A-PAT, PIT-A-PAT, comin on behind her. There's the wolf. He says to her, says, "You moved."

She says, "Oh, no, dear wolf, what occasion have I to move?"

"Sing that sweetest, goodest song again," says the big, bad wolf.

She sang:

"Tray bla-tray, tray bla-tray, tray-bla-cum qua, kimo."

The wolf is gone again.

And she, Little Daughter, *pit-a-pat, pit-a-pat, pit-a-pat*tin away home. She is so close to the gate now. And this time she hears PIT-A-PAT, PIT-A-PAT, PIT-A-PAT comin on *quick* behind her.

Little Daughter slips inside the gate. She shuts it—CRACK! PLICK!—right in that big, bad wolf's face.

She sweetest, goodest safe!

Ghabru and the Little Lie

PARTAP SHARMA

Little Ghabru was afraid of everyone and everything. So when he was asked anything, he always told a lie.

One day he wandered into a forest. An owl asked him, "Who are you?" Ghabru was about to tell a lie. But the wind said, "Hush," and Ghabru kept quiet.

Then a tiger growled, "Ghabru." Ghabru was about to say, "Not I," or "That's not my name." But the wind said, "Hush," and Ghabru kept quiet.

The owl flew down and said, "We're looking for you." And the tiger said, "Ghabru." But Ghabru kept quiet.

Ghabru walked on, and many animals wanted to speak to him, but he listened to the wind and his own fear and kept quiet.

"Why do they want to speak to me?" he wondered. "Why?"

Then a parrot flew down and said, "Ghabru! Ghabru! They've all heard about you because I told them. I listened at your window and repeated all you said. Now they all want to talk to you."

"Why?" Ghabru asked.

"Well, now, really," the parrot said, "I don't like gossiping, and I shouldn't really repeat what others have said, but you know what they're saying?"

"No," said Ghabru, shaking his head.

"Well, they're saying," and the parrot flapped his wings and jumped about and screeched, "Ghabru is a liar! Ghabru is a liar!"

Suddenly all the animals of the forest were standing in a circle around Ghabru, jumping up and down and shouting, "Ghabru is a liar! Ghabru is a liar!"

"I'm not," said Ghabru. "Why, I'm the only person in the whole world who's never told a lie."

When the animals heard this, they screamed with laughter and jumped up and down and sang in chorus, "Ghabru is a liar! Ghabru is a liar!"

"Poor boy!" the owl said when the others had stopped jumping and shouting. "Poor, poor boy. He's just afraid to say he doesn't know when he doesn't know, and when he does know something, he's afraid of speaking the truth."

"I'm not!" said Ghabru. "And I can prove it because I know everything. Go on. Ask me anything you like."

"All right," said the elephant. "Can you tell me why I have a trunk?"

"That's simple," said Ghabru. "You didn't always have a trunk, of course. You got it, like all people do, when preparing to go on a long journey."

The elephant trumpeted and the animals snorted and shouted, but the owl said, "Let's be fair to the boy. The elephant does, after all, use his trunk for carrying things."

But the animals jumped about and shouted, "Ghabru is a liar! Ghabru is a liar!"

"Justice," the owl said pompously, "must not only be merciful but must also guide and help the weak."

"Ghabru is not weak," the tiger growled. "Ask him. He'll say he's the strongest boy in the world."

"I hate to repeat it," the parrot said, "but Ghabru told another boy that the tiger got his stripes because Ghabru slapped him."

Even the owl hooted at this and could not help laughing.

"Really, Ghabru," the owl said, "you must be more careful what you say."

"He'd better be!" the wild boar snorted. "I'm told he called me the biggest bore in the world."

"Anyway," the owl said to Ghabru, "now we've told you how we feel. The tiger, the elephant, and the boar will show you the way home."

Ghabru didn't like the idea of walking along with a tiger, an elephant and a boar. He was afraid. He said, "I can find my own way home."

"Are you sure?" the owl asked.

"Of course," Ghabru said, lying.

Then he walked away. He had lied to his mother when he set out. He had said he was going to the bazaar but instead had wandered into the forest. Now it was getting dark, and Ghabru after a while realized that he definitely was lost.

"Lo-os-st," the wind seemed to mock at him.

"Tch tch tch tch," the crickets clicked in the night.

"What shall I do now?" Ghabru wondered and trembled. "No one will think of looking for me in the forest. They'll be searching the bazaar streets. That was such a silly little lie. Oh, that was such a silly little lie!"

The owl and the parrot found Ghabru shivering in the dark. The owl asked Ghabru if he was lost. But Ghabru was afraid to say he was lost because he didn't trust the owl or the parrot. He thought, "If I say I am lost, they'll lead me away to some place and kill me and eat me. I've got to pretend I can take care of myself."

The owl said, "We can send the parrot with a message. You know he can repeat whatever you say."

Ghabru looked angry and stamped his foot and said, "I'm *not* lost. I tell you I'm here. How can I be lost if I'm here and know I'm here?"

"Very well, then," said the owl and flew away. And the parrot flew to Ghabru's house and perched on the windowsill and repeated Ghabru's words, "I'm *not* lost. I tell you I'm here. How can I be lost if I'm here and know I'm here?"

Ghabru's mother and father heard this and exclaimed,
"Thank God, the boy is safe."

But though they searched the house, they couldn't find
Ghabru.

Once again, they searched outside and in the streets and called his name. And the parrot perched in the dark treetops and flew about the street, saying, "I'm *not* lost. I tell you I'm here. How can I be lost if I'm here and know I'm here?"

Many people of the town came out to search. They followed the voice about but saw no sign of Ghabru. Some said, "Something evil has happened to the boy. He's been turned invisible. We hear him but cannot see him."

Others said, "The boy is dead and it is his spirit speaking. This town is bewitched."

Finally, someone discovered it was the parrot speaking. But by now they were all so full of fear and superstition that they thought the boy had been turned into a parrot.

So they caught the parrot and prayed to it, and Ghabru's parents took the parrot home and treated it like their son. After the first little surprise at this turn of events, the parrot began to enjoy being petted and fussed over.

In the forest after a few hours, Ghabru could bear it no longer. He began to cry and shouted, "I'm lost! I'm lost! Help."

But no one was about, only the wind and the crickets clicking in the dark.

Two days later, hungry and wretched, Ghabru found his way home. He came in to find a number of people, including his father and mother, standing around the parrot and fussing over it. They were all calling the parrot "Ghabru".

"Here I am!" Ghabru said. And they all looked at him in amazement.

Just then the parrot said, "I'm *not* lost. I tell you I'm here. How can I be lost if I'm here and know I'm here?"

When Ghabru heard this, he realized at once what had happened. He ran to the parrot, kissed it, and said, "Go back and tell the animals that I shall try never to tell a lie again. Not even a little one."

The parrot flew away. And Ghabru said to his parents, "I was lost in the forest."

"Oh no, that can't be!" everyone said. They said, "Don't lie to us. We know you were bewitched and locked up in the body of a parrot."

"No, no!" Ghabru said. "I was just lost in the forest."

But they did not want to believe him. And Ghabru realized that telling the truth, though it is better, is often more difficult than telling a lie. And to this day the people of the town say Ghabru was locked up in the body of a parrot. And to this day, Ghabru insists that he was just lost in the forest.

The Cat and the Mouse in Partnership
THE BROTHERS GRIMM

A Cat had made acquaintance with a Mouse, and had spoken so much of the great love and friendship she felt for her, that at last the Mouse consented to live in the same house with her, and to go shares in the housekeeping. "But we must provide for the winter or else we shall suffer hunger," said the Cat. "You, little Mouse, cannot venture

everywhere in case you run at last into a trap." This good counsel was followed, and a little pot of fat was bought. But they did not know where to put it. At length, after long consultation, the Cat said, "I know of no place where it could be better put than in the church. No one will trouble to take it away from there. We will hide it in a corner, and we won't touch it till we are in want." So the little pot was placed in safety; but it was not long before the Cat had a great longing for it, and said to the Mouse, "I wanted to tell you, little Mouse, that my cousin has a little son, white with brown spots, and she wants me to be godmother to it. Let me go out today, and do you take care of the house alone."

"Yes, go certainly," replied the Mouse, "and when you eat anything good, think of me; I should very much like a drop of the red christening wine."

But it was all untrue. The Cat had no cousin, and had not been asked to be godmother. She went straight to the church, slunk to the little pot of fat, began to lick it, and licked the top off. Then she took a walk on the roofs of the town, looked at the view, stretched herself out in the sun, and licked her lips whenever she thought of the little pot of fat. As soon as it was evening she went home again.

"Ah, here you are again!" said the Mouse. "You must certainly have had an enjoyable day."

"It went off very well," answered the Cat.

"What was the child's name?" asked the Mouse.

"Top Off," said the Cat drily.

"Topoff!" echoed the Mouse. "It is indeed a wonderful and curious name. Is it in your family?"

"What is there odd about it?" said the Cat. "It is not worse than Breadthief, as your godchild is called."

Not long after this another great longing came over the Cat. She said to the Mouse, "You must again be kind enough to look after the house alone, for I have been asked a second time to stand godmother, and, as this child has a white ring round its neck, I cannot refuse."

The kind Mouse agreed, but the Cat slunk under the town wall to the church, and ate up half of the pot of fat. "Nothing tastes better," said she, "than what one eats by oneself," and she was very much pleased with her day's work. When she came home the Mouse asked, "What was this child called?"

"Half Gone," answered the Cat.

"Halfgone! What a name! I have never heard it in my life. I don't believe it is in the calendar."

Soon the Cat's mouth began to water once more after her licking business. "All good things in threes," she said to the Mouse. "I have again to stand godmother. The child is quite black, and has very white paws, but not a single white hair on its body. This only happens once in two years, so you will let me go out?"

"Topoff! Halfgone!" repeated the Mouse. "They are such curious names; they make me very thoughtful."

"Oh, you sit at home in your dark grey coat and your long tail," said the Cat, "and you get fanciful. That comes of not going out in the day."

The Mouse had a good cleaning out while the Cat was gone, and made the house tidy; but the greedy Cat ate the fat every bit up. "When it is all gone one can be at rest," she said to herself, and at night she came home sleek and satisfied. The Mouse asked at once after the third child's name.

"It won't please you any better," said the Cat. "He was called

Clean Gone."

"Cleangone!" repeated the Mouse. "I do not believe that name has been printed any more than the others. Cleangone! What can it mean?" She shook her head, curled herself up, and went to sleep.

From this time on no one asked the Cat to stand godmother; but when the winter came and there was nothing to be got outside, the Mouse remembered their provision and said, "Come, Cat, we will go to our pot of fat which we have stored away; it will taste very good."

"Yes, indeed," answered the Cat. "It will taste as good to you as if you stretched your thin tongue out of the window."

They started off, and when they reached it they found the pot in its place, but quite empty!

"Ah," said the Mouse, "now I know what has happened! It has all come out! You are a true friend to me! You have eaten it all when you stood godmother; first the top off, then half of it gone, then——"

"Will you be quiet!" screamed the Cat. "Another word and I will eat you up."

"Cleangone," was already on the poor Mouse's tongue, and scarcely was it out than the Cat made a spring at her, seized and swallowed her.

You see that is the way of the world.

The Strange Egg
MARGARET MAHY

Once Molly found a strange leathery egg in the swamp. She put it under Mrs Warm the broody hen to hatch it out. It hatched out into a sort of dragon.

Her father said, "This is no ordinary dragon. This is a dinosaur."

"What is a dinosaur?" asked Molly.

"Well," said her father, "a long time ago there were a lot of dinosaurs. They were all big lizards. Some of them were bigger than houses. They all died long ago. . . . All except this one," he added gloomily. "I hope it is not one of the larger meat-eating lizards as then it might grow up to worry the sheep."

The dinosaur followed Mrs Warm about. She scratched worms for it, but the dinosaur liked plants better.

"Ah," said Molly's father. "It is a plant-eating dinosaur —one of the milder kind. They are stupid but good-natured," he added.

Professors of all ages came from near and far to see Molly's dinosaur. She led it around on a string. Every day she needed a longer piece of string. The dinosaur grew as big as ten

68

elephants. It ate all the flowers in the garden and Molly's mother got cross.

"I am tired of having no garden and I am tired of making tea for all the professors," she said. "Let's send the dinosaur to the zoo."

"No," said Father. "The place wouldn't be the same without it."

So the dinosaur stayed. Mrs Warm used to perch on it every night. She had never before hatched such a grand successful egg.

One day it began to rain. . . . It rained and rained and rained and rained so heavily that the water in the river got deep and overflowed.

"A flood, a flood—we will drown," screamed Molly's mother.

"Hush, dear," said Molly's father. "We will ride to a safe place on Molly's dinosaur. Whistle to him, Molly."

Molly whistled and the dinosaur came towards her with Mrs Warm the hen, wet and miserable, on his back. Molly and her father and mother climbed on to the dinosaur's back with her. They held an umbrella over themselves and had warm drinks out of a thermos flask. Just as they left, the house was swept away by the flood.

"Well, dear, there you are," said Molly's father. "You see it was useful to have a dinosaur, after all. And I am now able to tell you that this is the biggest kind of dinosaur and its name is Brontosaurus."

Molly was pleased to think her pet had such a long, dignified-sounding name. It matched him well. As they went along they rescued a lot of other people climbing trees and house tops, and floating on chicken crates and fruit boxes. They rescued cats

and dogs, two horses and an elephant which was floating away
from a circus. The dinosaur paddled on cheerfully. By the time
they came in sight of dry land, his back was quite crowded. On
the land policemen were getting boats ready to go looking for
people, but all the people were safe on the dinosaur's back.

After the flood went down and everything was as it should be, a fine medal was given to Molly's dinosaur as most heroic animal of the year and many presents were given to him.

The biggest present of all was a great big swimming-pool made of rubber so you could blow it up. It was so big it took one man nearly a year to blow it up. It was a good size for dinosaurs of the Brontosaurus type. He lived in the swimming-pool after that (and Molly's mother was able to grow her flowers again). It is well known that Brontosauruses like to swim and paddle. It took the weight off his feet. Mrs Warm the hen used to swim with him a bit, and it is not very often you find a swimming hen.

So you see this story has a happy ending after all, which is not easy with a pet as big as ten elephants. And just to end the story I must tell you that though Molly's dinosaur had the long name of Brontosaurus, Molly always called it "Rosie".

Micky and the Macaroni

ITALIAN

One day Micky's mother sent him out to gather herbs in the wood. "While you're gone," she said, "I'll cook some good macaroni for dinner. Come back quickly." But Micky stayed out playing in the woods; and by the time he had come back the other children had eaten up nearly all the macaroni. So she put the little that was left into a basin of broth, and set it before him. But Micky was sulky and shoved it aside, saying if that was all they had left him for dinner he wouldn't eat anything at all.

Then his mother called out to the Stick in the corner, "Stick, Stick, beat Micky. Micky won't eat his macaroni." The Stick paid no heed. So she cried, "Fire, Fire, burn Stick. Stick won't beat Micky. Micky won't eat his macaroni." The Fire paid no attention. So she cried, "Water, Water, quench Fire. Fire won't burn Stick. Stick won't beat Micky. Micky won't eat his macaroni." Not a bit of heed did the Water pay. So she called again, "Ox, Ox, drink Water. Water won't quench Fire. Fire won't burn Stick. Stick won't beat Micky. Micky won't eat his macaroni." The Ox was deaf. So once again she cried, "Rope,

Rope, bind Ox! Ox won't drink Water. Water won't quench
Fire. Fire won't burn Stick. Stick won't beat Micky. Micky
won't eat his macaroni!" The Rope paid no heed. So she cried
out, "Mousie, Mousie, gnaw Rope! Rope won't bind Ox. Ox
won't drink Water. Water won't quench Fire. Fire won't burn

Stick. Stick won't beat Micky. Micky won't eat his macaroni."
But the Mouse would not stir. So she called, "Cat, Cat, gobble
Mousie. Mousie won't gnaw Rope. Rope won't bind Ox. Ox
won't drink Water. Water won't quench Fire. Fire won't burn
Stick. Stick won't beat Micky. Micky won't eat his macaroni."

But the Cat was not deaf. The Cat sprang up and began to gobble the Mouse. The Mouse began to gnaw the Rope. The Rope began to bind the Ox. The Ox began to drink the Water. The Water began to quench the Fire. The Fire began to burn the Stick. The Stick began to beat Micky. Micky began to eat his macaroni; and he ate it to the end.

The Hole in the Sky
POLISH

Once upon a time there was a little tailor called Joseph Nitechka, who was so slender you could thread him through one of his own needles. He was so thin he could eat nothing but noodles, as they were the only food narrow enough to go down his throat. But he was a merry man and a handsome one too.

He lived contentedly in the town of Taidaraida, until one day a gypsy came to ask for his help. She had cut her foot and he stitched her skin so neatly that no scar showed. To thank him, the delighted gypsy told his fortune from the palm of his hand.

"If you leave Taidaraida on Sunday and always walk to the West you will come to a town where you will be made King," she said.

Nitechka laughed and didn't believe her. But that night the tailor dreamt he became such a rich King he grew as round as a barrel. He woke up and thought, "Who knows? Maybe I will become King if I go Westwards." So he packed a hundred needles, a thousand miles of thread, an iron and a pair of huge scissors and set off. But he did not know where the West was and no one else in Taidaraida could tell him either.

At last he asked an ancient man of one hundred and six years old, who pondered and replied, "The West must be where the sun sets." He seemed so wise, the tailor went where he said. Suddenly a gust of wind lifted Nitechka off his feet—because he was so very thin—and wafted him away. Nitechka laughed

with pleasure and floated along for many miles until the wind threw him abruptly into the arms of a scarecrow. This scarecrow was very elegant. He had a tail coat, a stove-pipe hat and slightly torn trousers. His hands and feet were made of sticks. Nitechka bowed low and said in his thin voice, "I am truly sorry if I trod on your foot, your honour. I am Mr Nitechka, the tailor."

"Delighted to make your acquaintance," answered the scarecrow. "I am Count Scarecrow and my coat of arms is four sticks. I watch the birds to see they don't steal the corn, but they don't interest me. I am unusually brave and I like to fight lions and tigers. However, they rarely come to eat the corn. Where are you travelling?"

"I am going West to a place where I shall be made King. Would you like to come with me Count Scarecrow?"

"Well I'm bored of staying here, so I'll come. But please mend my clothes before we go. I must look respectable as I might get married on the way."

Nitechka obligingly worked away and soon the scarecrow's clothes and hat looked like new. The birds tittered at Count Scarecrow as he strode proudly away with the tailor.

He and Nitechka soon became great friends. At night they slept in the fields and Nitechka tied himself to the scarecrow in case the wind blew him away again. When they were attacked by dogs, Count Scarecrow, who was brave by profession, tore off his foot and threw it at them. Then he would pick up the foot and tie it on again.

One evening they saw light shining from a house in a wood.

"Maybe we can stay the night there," said the tailor.

"Certainly, let us do them the honour," answered Count Scarecrow.

When they came closer they saw the house was a strange one. It had four feet and was turning round and round. "This house must belong to a cheerful man. He never stops dancing," whispered Nitechka.

They waited until the door came round to them and entered. It was an extraordinary place. Although it was summer there was a blazing stove on which a nobleman sat warming himself, occasionally eating a glowing coal with relish. He bowed and to their amazement said, "Mr Nitechka and Count Scarecrow, I presume. You are welcome to stay tonight and dine with my family."

At this a large party appeared. The nobleman's daughter was beautiful, but she laughed like a neighing horse. When they sat down to eat, Nitechka and Count Scarecrow sat on a bench, but all the others sat on braziers of hot coals. "Our family always feels the cold," their host explained. Nitechka was just about to sip some thick black soup, when Count Scarecrow hissed in his ear, "Don't drink it – it is hot pitch!" Pretending to enjoy it, they poured the soup under the table. The next course was rats in black sauce, followed by fried locusts, spaghetti made of worms and for pudding, rotten eggs. Nitechka and the scarecrow, feeling more and more scared, dropped everything under the table.

"Did you know, Mr Nitechka, that the King has just died in Pacanów?" asked their host.

"Is that far away?" asked the tailor.

"Two days away as the crow flies. And did you know that whoever marries my daughter will become King there?" His daughter neighed loudly at this and embraced Nitechka.

"We must escape!" whispered Count Scarecrow.

"But we can't find the door when the house is dancing round like this!" answered Nitechka. Then their host asked Nitechka for a song. The tailor stood up and sang the only song he knew in his thin reedy voice. It was a hymn to the Virgin Mary, and as soon as they heard it the whole family rose up, shouting and cursing. But Nitechka kept on singing, although the house was now running away with them. He started to sing the song again as soon as it was finished and immediately everything vanished, leaving Nitechka and Count Scarecrow sitting alone in a field.

"Thank goodness we overcame those wicked devils," said the tailor.

"I scared them off!" boasted the scarecrow.

Seven days later they arrived at the beautiful town of Paca-nów, where the King had died. All around was sunshine, but over the town itself the rain bucketed down from the sky. The townspeople saw the two friends and ran towards them, led by the Burgomaster riding on a goat.

"Please help us!" they said. "Since our King died it has been pouring with rain. We cannot make fires because the water floods down the chimneys and we shall die of cold! Also the King's daughter can't stop crying and this makes even more water! But she has vowed to marry anyone who can stop the rain and then he will become King."

"We will try to help," said Nitechka. He and Count Scarecrow were led into the town and everyone gathered round full of hope. But although Nitechka and Count Scarecrow thought for three days, they couldn't decide how to stop the rain.

Suddenly Nitechka bleated with excitement, "I know where the rain comes from!"

"Where?"

"From the sky."

"I know that," said Count Scarecrow. "It doesn't fall up-wards, does it?"

"No, but why does it fall only on the town?"

"Because everywhere else the weather is sunny."

"Don't be a fool, Count," said the tailor. "How long has it rained?"

"Since the King died."

"That's it! The King was so great that when he died and went up to heaven, he made a huge hole in the sky! The rain pours through and will never stop unless the hole is sewn up!"

In great excitement Nitechka and Count Scarecrow ex-plained to the people of Pacanów how the tailor would stop the rain. "Long live Nitechka!" shouted everyone. The tailor asked for all the ladders in the town to be tied together and leant against the sky. He took his hundred needles, threaded one and climbed up and up. Count Scarecrow stood below and unwound a spool of thread a thousand miles long. At the top Nitechka found an enormous tear in the sky as large as Pacanów, with rain pouring through. He stitched and stitched for two days without stopping. Then he pressed the sky with his iron and climbed down, exhausted.

The sun shone again over Pacanów, the princess dried her eyes and kissed Nitechka. Then the Burgomaster and the people brought him a golden crown. Everyone cried, "Long Live King Nitechka, husband of our princess!"

So the merry tailor married the princess and was crowned King. He reigned long and happily and the rain never fell on his kingdom. But he never forgot his comrade, Count Scarecrow. Nitechka made him Grand Warden of the kingdom, and every day he drove away birds from the King's head.

Mr Miacca

JOSEPH JACOBS

Tommy Grimes was sometimes a good boy, and sometimes a bad boy; and when he was a bad boy, he was a very bad boy. Now his mother used to say to him: "Tommy, Tommy, be a good boy, and don't go out of the street, or else Mr Miacca will take you." But still when he was a bad boy he would go out of the street; and one day, sure enough, he had scarcely got round the corner, when Mr Miacca did catch him and popped him into a bag upside down, and took him off to his house.

When Mr Miacca got Tommy inside, he pulled him out of the bag and sat him down, and felt his arms and legs. "You're rather tough," says he; "but you're all I've got for supper, and you'll not taste bad boiled. But body o' me, I've forgot the herbs, and it's bitter you'll taste without herbs. Sally! Here, I say, Sally!" and he called Mrs Miacca.

So Mrs Miacca came out of another room and said: "What d'ye want, my dear?"

"Oh, here's a little boy for supper," said Mr Miacca, "and I've forgot the herbs. Mind him, will ye, while I go for them."

"All right, my love," says Mrs Miacca, and off he goes.

Then Tommy Grimes said to Mrs Miacca: "Does Mr Miacca always have little boys for supper?"

"Mostly, my dear," said Mrs Miacca, "if little boys are bad enough, and get in his way."

"And don't you have anything else but boy-meat? No pudding?" asked Tommy.

"Ah, I loves pudding," says Mrs Miacca. "But it's not often the likes of me gets pudding."

"Why, my mother is making a pudding this very day," said Tommy Grimes, "and I am sure she'd give you some, if I ask her. Shall I run and get some?"

"Now, that's a thoughtful boy," said Mrs Miacca, "only don't be long and be sure to be back for supper."

So off Tommy pelted, and right glad he was to get off so cheap; and for many a long day he was as good as good could be, and never went round the corner of the street. But he couldn't always be good; and one day he went round the corner, and as luck would have it, he hadn't scarcely got round it when Mr Miacca grabbed him up, popped him in his bag, and took him home.

When he got him there, Mr Miacca dropped him out; and when he saw him, he said: "Ah, you're the youngster that served me and my missus such a shabby trick, leaving us without any supper. Well, you shan't do it again. I'll watch over you myself. Here, get under the sofa, and I'll sit on it and watch the pot boil for you."

So poor Tommy Grimes had to creep under the sofa, and Mr Miacca sat on it and waited for the pot to boil. And they waited and they waited, but still the pot didn't boil, till at last Mr Miacca got tired of waiting, and he said: "Here, you under there, I'm not going to wait any longer; put out your leg, and I'll stop your giving us the slip."

So Tommy put out a leg and Mr Miacca got a chopper, and chopped it off, and pops it in the pot.

Suddenly he calls out: "Sally, my dear, Sally!" and nobody answered. So he went into the next room to look out for Mrs Miacca, and while he was there Tommy crept out from under the sofa and ran out of the door. For it was a leg of the sofa that he had put out.

So Tommy Grimes ran home, and he never went round the corner again till he was old enough to go alone.

The Wonderful Cake-Horse

TERRY JONES

Aman once made a cake shaped like a horse. That night a shooting star flew over the house and a spark happened to fall on the cake-horse. Well, the cake-horse lay there for a few moments. Then it gave a snort. Then it whinnied, scrambled to its legs, and shook its mane of white icing, and stood there in the moonlight, gazing round at the world.

The man, who was asleep in bed, heard the noise and looked out of the window, and saw his cake-horse running around the garden, bucking and snorting, just as if it had been a real wild horse.

"Hey! Cake-horse!" cried the man. "What are you doing?"

"Aren't I a fine horse!" cried the cake-horse. "You can ride me if you like."

But the man said: "You've got no horse-shoes and you've got no saddle, and you're only made of cake!"

The cake-horse snorted and bucked and kicked the air, and galloped across the garden, and leapt clean over the gate, and disappeared into the night.

The next morning, the cake-horse arrived in the nearby town, and went to the blacksmith and said: "Blacksmith, make me some good horse-shoes, for my feet are only made of cake."

But the blacksmith said: "How will you pay me?"

And the cake-horse answered: "If you make me some horse-shoes, I'll be your friend."

But the blacksmith shook his head: "I don't need friends like that!" he said.

So the cake-horse galloped to the saddler, and said: "Saddler! Make me a saddle of the best leather – one that will go with my icing-sugar mane!"

But the saddler said: "If I make you a saddle, how will you pay me?"

"I'll be your friend," said the cake-horse.

"I don't need friends like that!" said the saddler and shook his head.

The cake-horse snorted and bucked and kicked its legs in the air and said: "Why doesn't anyone want to be my friend? I'll go and join the wild horses!" And he galloped out of the town and off to the moors where the wild horses roamed.

But when he saw the other wild horses, they were all so big and wild that he was afraid they would trample him to crumbs without even noticing he was there.

Just then he came upon a mouse who was groaning to himself under a stone.

"What's the matter with you?" asked the cake-horse.

"Oh," said the mouse, "I ran away from my home in the

town, and came up here where there is nothing to eat, and now I'm dying of hunger and too weak to get back."

The cake-horse felt very sorry for the mouse, so it said: "Here you are! You can nibble a bit of me, if you like, for I'm made of cake."

"That's most kind of you," said the mouse, and he ate a little of the cake-horse's tail, and a little of his icing-sugar mane. "Now I feel much better."

Then the cake-horse said: "If only I had a saddle and some horse-shoes, I could carry you back to the town."

"*I'll* make you them," said the mouse, and he made four little horse-shoes out of acorn-cups, and a saddle out of beetle-shells, and he got up on the cake-horse's back and rode him back to town.

And there they remained the best of friends for the rest of their lives.